Inspiration
When You Need It

© 2010 Patsy S.C. Jud

All rights reserved.

No parts of this book may be reproduced,
stored, or copied without the expressed written
consent of the author.

ISBN: 978-0-9790993-3-5

Library of Congress Copyright Pending

Inspiration
When You Need It

Poetry by Patsy S.C. Jud
Photography by Kenneth F. Hilliard

 Sheema Publishing, LLC
sheemapublishing@sbcglobal.net

Dedication

To all who have inspired, loved and supported us.

A special thank you to Jeannie Krupp for helping edit these poems.

A special thank you to Mark Springer, II for helping edit "Images in a Cloud"

Photographic Table of Contents

Front Cover: An inspiring Sweetgum seedling having faith it will grow on a boulder in the middle of the Little Tennessee River, Bryson City, North Carolina

Back Cover: Classic barn photo blending rustic charm with colorful new flowers at Rennie Orchards near Traverse City, Michigan

First Page: Fall color on a clear day with Clingman's Dome in the background 34 miles to the north in Great Smokey Mountains National Park, North Carolina

Associated Poems

Yes…I Know: Sun setting over Lake Michigan and lighthouse at Benton Harbor… shamans believe sunset is a time for reflection of the events of the day......................2

Behind Every Roadblock Lies and Opportunity: View through a Roman Arch of the Italian coastline along the Ligurian Sea… the arch allows you to peer through stone walls to really 'see' the people you should know 10

Your Life is What You Want it to Be: Ignoring stubborn snow, feisty spring flowers near Marcellus, Michigan have decided it's time to grow...................................... 12

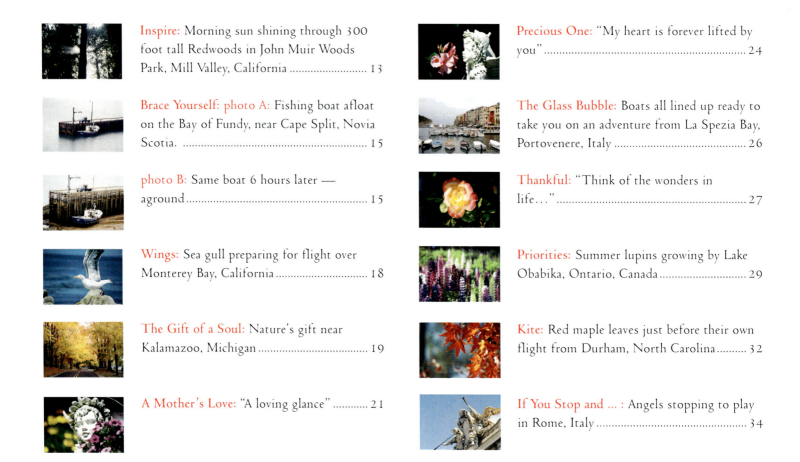

Inspire: Morning sun shining through 300 foot tall Redwoods in John Muir Woods Park, Mill Valley, California 13

Brace Yourself: photo A: Fishing boat afloat on the Bay of Fundy, near Cape Split, Novia Scotia. 15

photo B: Same boat 6 hours later — aground 15

Wings: Sea gull preparing for flight over Monterey Bay, California 18

The Gift of a Soul: Nature's gift near Kalamazoo, Michigan 19

A Mother's Love: "A loving glance" 21

Precious One: "My heart is forever lifted by you" 24

The Glass Bubble: Boats all lined up ready to take you on an adventure from La Spezia Bay, Portovenere, Italy 26

Thankful: "Think of the wonders in life…" 27

Priorities: Summer lupins growing by Lake Obabika, Ontario, Canada 29

Kite: Red maple leaves just before their own flight from Durham, North Carolina 32

If You Stop and … : Angels stopping to play in Rome, Italy 34

If Only for a Moment: "Catching" a sunset over Lake Michigan 35

How to Make a Difference: Timed release irrigation in early Spring on farm near Cassapolis, Michigan 37

Faith: An inspiring Sweetgum seedling having faith it will grow on a boulder in the middle of the Little Tennessee River, Bryson City, North Carolina 39

For Today: September 11, 2001: Dancing mist on the Little Tennessee River, Bryson City, North Carolina 41

Everyday: Another sunset from the Pacific Coast Highway overlooking Bodega Bay, California 44

Happiness: Bubbles of laughter as water playfully dashes by on the Nantahalla River, Wesser, North Carolina 46

A Life Worth Living: Enduring Sequoia standing tall in Sequoia National Park, California 48

My Wish for You: Rainbow over Niagara Falls, New York 49

The Value of a Dime: Providing wealth and health, Nobile grapes in vineyard near Montepulciano, Italy 51

I Believe in You: The remarkable "Lone Cypress Tree" overlooking Carmel Bay near Pebble Beach, California 53

How to Measure the Life of a Man: Wise old El Capitan standing tall over the Merced River, Yosemite National Park, California 56

Anchored into a boulder, this young tree has survived an early spring flood on the Little Tennessee River near Bryson City, North Carolina 59

Yes I know……

Yes I know you are scared
The unknown is hard to face
Your strength will carry you

Yes I know you are angry
It is okay to be upset
Your good outlook will return

Yes I know you hurt
The pain will get better
You are under good care

Yes I know you are loved
Many want to see you at your best
You can reach out for help

Yes I know you are strong
Reach for inspiration around you
Your inner guide will help

Yes I know this is difficult
Life's challenges make us better
You will persevere

Yes I know you are not alone
I am here for you
You have a friend

Images in a Cloud

By Patsy S.C. Jud

*To understand my inspiration,
it is important to know my story.*

"Have you heard of someone who has had her head completely detached from her body, structurally, and lived to tell about it? Patsy that is you."

I was in the park looking up at the clouds when a warm breeze came and stroked my bare feet.

She visits the doctor in 1996 and her life is forever changed. Serious neck and shoulder pain has brought her to the emergency room, to physical therapists, and to two doctor visits within the last four months. All diagnose her condition as tight muscles, until this day. A doctor notices Patsy holding her head forward and takes an x-ray. He sees serious neck damage but cannot diagnose the cause without further tests to narrow it down. As a precaution, he places her in a cervical-thoracic neck brace. The brace limits neck and upper body movement, she turns her entire body to look a direction. The doctors have never seen a condition like hers before and they are baffled by it. Within one week she is told that she may have a broken neck, a bone disease, a genetic abnormality, or cancer.

In the space of eight days she has two surgeries. The first is a biopsy needed for diagnosis. The radiologist tells her this procedure is the most painful one performed by radiology because numbing bone is impossible. Her tolerance to pain is so high the biopsy is not so bad. The biopsy diagnoses a hemangioma tumor, a benign vascular tumor that is characteristically a skin abnormality and rarely is seen inside the body. Her neck is too unstable to remove the tumor. The second surgery is an ethanol injection needed to cut off the blood supply and starve the tumor.

My wish is to live a long and loving life.

The tumor causes damage to her neck that is so extensive that movement of her head makes quadro-paralysis likely. The tumor causes her spinal cord to be unprotected and leaves several nerve roots dangling. She is put into traction: a vice is screwed into her skull and a twenty-five pound sandbag is attached. The purpose of traction is to stretch her neck muscles and to make neck surgery possible. The nurses tell her that the most weight they have seen on a person before is ten pounds, and that was on a leg. Her body instantly rejects any pain medication. The doctors do not know why, but later she learns it is a drug-to-drug interaction between the morphine and ethanol alcohol. For the next twenty hours she is a mess lying on her back with uncontrolled nausea that continuously covers her. She cries. It is the weight, the pain, and the knowledge she might die before she turns twenty-one. Dr. Jones, a neck specialist at the Presbyterian St. Lukes Medical Center in Denver, CO and her chief surgeon, understands her fear. "I have called all over the nation trying to find a way to fix you," he tells her. "I believe that this next surgery is what will give you the greatest chance for a normal life. Though many specialists are skeptical if you can survive, I believe that you can because you have the greatest attitude I have ever seen."

Why is it that other students are looking forward to Homecoming and taking tests, and I am in here facing a life-threatening battle?

The surgery lasts twelve hours. The damage to her spine is so extensive the surgeons fall silent. The hemangioma tumor had deteriorated two vertebrae completely and left remnants of two others. The surgery entails spinal reconstruction with a bridge of titanium, a wire pulley, and screws built over ten vertebrae, nerve repair, and hours of bone grafts from the hip. Against the numerous odds she survives.

I remember looking at my right hand: it was so swollen that it looked like a balloon and no matter how hard I tried, it wouldn't move.

It is over. Dr. Jones is ecstatic at the initial results of the surgery. She wonders if she can move her legs. She is afraid to try, but she forces herself. When her legs move no words can describe her elation or relief. Swelling from the traction and surgery has left her face unrecognizable. Dr. Jones is worried that she has lost the movement of her right hand. She is placed in intensive care. As she lies there, fighting for her life, a doctor gives her morphine and the nausea returns. She tries to hold it in but cannot. A tired nurse comes to take her blood and yells at her to quit throwing up. She feels defeated.

Maybe being bionic will come in handy. I wonder if Matthew McConaughey has kissed a bionic woman?

That night is the longest of her life. Even the traction does not compare to this. She prays to die.

She thinks of her friends and family. She realizes her energy has been focused on protecting them and herself from this moment. She reassured them at every turn. She told them if she had cancer, she wanted to be a Cancer Camp Counselor. If she were paralyzed, she could become a motivational speaker. She did not tell them about the pain. She did not tell them how hard it was to face the possibility of paralysis or death. She did not tell them she was scared. Her bravery has been as much for them as for her. But on this night her courage fails.

Help me to get better and to have the pain go away.

At last dawn comes and with the sunrise comes a new will to fight. She is able to move her right hand if only a little. With relief, Dr. Jones tells her that the radial nerve in her arm has only been bruised and that she will regain movement. With each passing hour her determination grows and when the physical therapist comes on the third day to help her sit, she stands. Her goal for the next day is to walk two steps. Instead she finds the strength to walk the length of the hall. At the end of the hall she finds Esperanza's room. The nurses have told her about Esperanza, a twenty-five-year-old who had neck damage in a car accident.

I cannot express what a blessing my family and friends are to me. They mean the world.

With nightfall the pain intensifies. A nurse suggests Extra-Strength Tylenol. Finally she relents with the hope that the medicine will bring relief not more nausea. She takes the pill with a cracker, the first solid food she's eaten in days. She feels fine but she's afraid she will be sick. The fear builds until it is almost a certainty. An orderly hears her crying and comes to check on her. His few words of encouragement have the power to put her fear to rest. She sleeps.

My nurse was laughing at me because I had tight muscles and after I took a muscle relaxer I told him my muscles were just hanging out going Do-Da-Do.

Her recovery quickens. The Tylenol provides enough relief that she can once again enjoy simple things like watching soccer games on TV simply because the men are hot. Every day each nurse comes in to say "Hello." She makes more frequent visits to Esperenza and her family says, "You have given our daughter so much joy and inspiration!"

Maybe that is why I went through this…to help Esperenza.

Eight days later she is discharged from the hospital. Dr. Jones removes forty staples from her back and sends her home in the brace again.

At home she decides to begin therapy on her own. Each morning she wakes and tells herself, "If I can walk down the hallway one more time than yesterday, the pain will be less." She is beginning to do things she had not been able to do for a long time. Two weeks later she sits through her sister's guitar concert. It is an accomplishment to sit so long without having to lie on the floor every five minutes to relieve the pain. It is the most enjoyable thing she can imagine.

I decided today that I am going to ride an elephant someday because I never have.

The long struggle of her recovery has come to an end. Almost a year later, she stands on the balcony of her new apartment, ecstatic at the prospect of returning to college. She no longer needs to have her mother shower her. She wears the neck brace only at night. He life is hers again.

The phone rings. It is Dr. Jones. He tells her fusion has captured and fused a normal vertebra. He fears that because she is so young there will be too much pressure on her normal vertebrae. Another operation is necessary. She keeps her composure long enough to hang up the phone and call her mother, but when she hears her mother's voice she lets it all out.

Dr. Jones told me that, in all of his years of practice, he has never seen so much damage to a neck nor has he had such a great patient.

She is in the hospital again. Once again she copes with the possibility of paralysis. Her sister strokes her hair and sings to her before Dr. Jones takes her to surgery. Dr. Jones uses a bone saw to free the fused normal vertebra and takes more bone grafts from her hip to strengthen the original ten-vertebrae fusion. The four-hour operation is a success and gives her neck more mobility.

The next day she convinces the doctor to discharge her. Her parents drive her home. In the car she tells them, "I am the bravest person that I know." Her father is silent but in his tears she sees he is thinking the same thing.

I love life with all my heart-except for the part of my heart that is taken in loving others.

She has missed a week of classes. She does not feel up to returning to school, but she is already behind. Her courses in Physics, Organic Chemistry, and Genetics cannot allow her to get more behind. The semester becomes more difficult as she suffers with reoccurring migraine headaches. Determination carries her. The headaches make it difficult to concentrate during final exams. She is disappointed she cannot perform her best. She realizes that even though she is bionic she is not invincible.

From today on I am sleeping well, eating right, exercising, and really taking care of myself…so I can enjoy life completely.

Eight-years later I write this essay with a racing mind. I am scared that a small accident could prevent me from living the life I want to. I am determined to work hard and to make each day its best. I am sad I will never again enjoy rollerblading or satisfy the expectations of a young nephew wanting to be picked up and held. I am disciplined to know what I can handle. I listen to my body. I am thankful for the encouragement my family has given me. I am blessed by the grace of God. I am appreciative to Dr. Jones for having the courage to study, try a new operation, and for his faith in me. I am ecstatic to have Brad Jud as a partner and for his unconditional love. I am proud of my Bachelor's Degree in Biology, Master's Degree in Business Administration, and career as a Pharmaceutical Representative. I enjoy motivational speaking. I am thankful for my life and my beautiful neck.

I know that our attitude and expectations are often the limitations that hold us back, more than anything else. My attitude prompted Dr. Jones to want to help me. My ability to focus on helping others allowed me to cope with my struggle. My faith carried me through my trial. I know what it is like to face your worst day head on. My life is my responsibility. I work hard everyday to exercise, eat right, and sleep well. I manage minimal neck pain by taking care of myself and continuing my own physical therapy. I know life is too short to wait for tomorrow.

No matter how bad life gets, there is someone who has it worse. Appreciate the good things you do have.

I look out the window at the clouds. As a child I believed that when you died you became a cloud and floated over the ones that you loved. I wish to become the biggest and fluffiest cloud that I can.

I know it is possible.

Behind a Roadblock Lies an Opportunity

When you are beaten by a stick
and life throws a curve ball
Do not think of it as a bad thing,
it is really not that at all

Opportunities are sometimes masked,
by a road that's hard to travel
When you focus on the positive,
the large rocks suddenly turn to gravel

The gravel turns to pebbles
as you learn and grow
The people who are supportive
are the people you should know

The pebbles are broken into grains of sand
As you increase your education
and lend a helping hand

The road may contain hills,
you do not wish to climb
Your strength will carry you,
a new understanding you will find

Love yourself enough
to not take the wrong road
Help others along the way
who are carrying a heavy load

Your road is unique
from each and every person you meet
Make your road the most amazing you can
and never admit defeat

Your Life is What You Want it to Be

Have you ever looked at someone and said
"Wow! What an easy life."
He has nice clothes, a great car,
and check out his wife.

Then you looked at your own life
and thought in shame
"Gee, he really has it all.
I wish my life could be the same."

The truth is, your life is what you want it to be.
Life is so much greater when you think positively

When you appreciate the sunsets,
a smile and the stars
You do not worry about what he thinks,
or if it's weird to love Mars

Loving who you are is an important thing
When you have that love,
it doesn't matter if your walk has a swing

Do not be hard on yourself
for not being the perfect man
No one is perfect, some just think,
"Yes, I can!"

That person is you, if you truly believe
"I am a great person.
There is nothing I cannot achieve."

Inspire

Where do you look for inspiration?
Movies, books, or dear loved ones

Does it come from stories of people passed by
Visions of the future unseen by the naked eye

Take a moment to think of what inspires you
With that inspiration think of all that you can do

You can achieve beyond your wildest dreams
Be the person who is kind and never mean

You can help others make their wishes come true
Take the moment to thank those who inspire you

You can fight to make this world a better place
Or take the time to put a smile on another's face

Live your life with passion, enjoy everything you do
For Inspiration can come from within a person like
YOU

Brace Yourself

When you must wear a neck brace
to hold up your dainty head
Do not think of it as the end of the world
But try these techniques instead

When others ask what happened here's what you do
Have a great time and come up with a story or two

Say, I was mountain biking one glorious day
When a grizzly bear came running my way
I peddled as fast as I could, then I hit a rock
I flew 52.3 feet, broke my neck and lost a sock

When people say,
"That is amazing and pat you on the back"
Just say, "Boy was I ever lucky to have some Boy
Scouts up there with packs"

Say, "I am just keeping my chin-up" or "You'll have to
brace yourself for this one."
Make the absolute most of this time
Wearing a brace can be fun

I know it is uncomfortable, frustrating,
and people like to stare
Just hold your head high
It is you who should not care
For you are very lucky to only have to wear a brace
There are many reasons to have a smile on your face

Tell yourself, "If I take care,
I will not have to wear this much longer."
Because of this experience, you are definitely stronger.
So brace yourself for a great future ahead
Realize there are many worse things to dread.

Wings

Have you ever wondered
what it would be like to have wings

To fly with no restrictions, no judgments

To do Aerial stunts without fear of being hurt

To know you are protected

To fly over all you love and to give them joy

To watch over and protect them
the way you have always dreamed

To float in comfort

To feel complete love and warmth

To be grateful to those who always gave you
acceptance, love, and warmth

Some may never understand

Why I received wings today

May they always know my wings gave me freedom

I will always be flying over them
and doing what I can to lift them up

This is why I fly

The Gift of a Soul

How do you determine the worth of a soul
Is it someone who strives to reach her own goal

Is the worth of a soul measured by its works for others
By caring compassion
of the Lord's sisters and brothers

What if the worth of a soul was put into "All for One"
Teaching others to care for themselves and to have fun

A willingness to give everything
to build a bridge together
A light that helps others in a storm to weather

The worth of a soul is measured in many ways
Remember it is up to you on how you spend your days

To spend moments with focus on others
To be the role model you found in your mother

To take the unique beauty within the heart of you
To use that passion to see your own challenges through

It is important to be proud of the worth of your soul
The Lord gave you gifts that move mountains
This you should know

A Mother's Love

A knowing glance: one who knows your sorrow
even when you try to hide it

A smile: encouragement and faith in your abilities
like no other

Trust: in you to do what is right
and to be true to yourself

Comfort: throughout struggles and tears the
knowledge tomorrow will be better

Joy: in watching you grow, develop and find your way

Wisdom: take the time to listen,
her years will enrich your life

Special: a way to make you feel as if you are the most
important person in the world

Laughter: at life's funny moments,
take time to enjoy them

Food: Mom's home cooked meals warm your spirit

A touch: in your heart, mind, and life,
it is always there

Strength: to help you through hard days

Love: beyond any you have known,
Love always makes the world better

Precious One

You make people smile just by being you
My heart strings tug with every little coo

Your laughter melts every inch of my soul
Your gaze around shows you really know

You go from 0-60 in a matter of seconds
You go from 60-0 when your need is met

You listen to music with deep attention
Your kicking coordination I can also mention

You are a joy I love every second it's true
My heart is forever lifted by you

The Glass Bubble

You cannot live life in a glass bubble,
is what I always say
It is my philosophy, I use it day by day

The world is an open book, with so many things to see
Adventures are behind each door, just waiting for me

There are many people with amazing stories to tell
I am not afraid to meet them or get to know them well

There is vast knowledge I need to be taught
And an awesome guy, just waiting to be caught

There are many mountains, left to be climbed
Many unwritten poems yet to be rhymed

There are sunsets to watch with people whom I love
Oceans to look upon from an airplane up above

There are frustrations that need to pass me by
There are tears I still need to cry

Like everyone, fears I do carry
A small fall could hurt me, and the dark seems scary

Despite these, I keep plugging along
Happy to walk, swim, and jam to my favorite song

To me life is an adventure
and around each corner or bend
Is the opportunity to smile
and shake the hand of a friend

You cannot live life in a glass bubble
there is way too much to do
The meaning of life is to live
and make your dreams come true

Thankful

On those days where life does not go right
The store was closed and you witnessed a fight
It drains you

A day where no matter what you do
It seems someone is out to get you
You are tired

On days like these you have the choice
To go with the flow or raise your voice
In Thanks

Think of all the things you are thankful for
Your wonderful baby or shiny floor
It lifts

Think of the wonders in life you have
Your handsome husband and great Mom and Dad
Enjoy them

Think of your good health and great friends
Of how this is the beginning and not the end
What a blessing

If you take the moment to give thanks today
You will find it easier to say
Life is not bad

Priorities

At the end of the day as you lie in bed
What thoughts fill your head
Are they thoughts of joy, the blessings of life
Or thoughts of work or the latest strife
Your thoughts can help you feel good throughout the day
If you take the initiative to prioritize and say
This is important

To make others feel at their best and not their worst
Make those who care feel appreciated and like they are first
To take time for you and to Thank the Lord above
To make others feel admired and your home filled with love
To feel good about the day passed by
With precious time spent with your little guy

At the end of the day your priorities will give way to

What you have at the end of life

Kite

Have you ever wondered what it would be like to be a kite
To soar above the sky with all your might

To feel like you are in control of the string that binds you
To look around at the world beside you

To do tricks that make people laugh with glee
To look down at the earth peacefully

To float around without a care
To have bright colors where people like to stare

Being a kite is not that bad
A great thought from a wonderful Mom and Dad

If You Stop and …

If you stop and listen to Italy, you will hear hundreds
of birds chirping, later frogs croaking.
The joyful sound of children
happy to be out of school.
If you stop and listen.

Two gentlemen walking the streets of Pienze in joyful
conversation, singing as only Italians can do.
The soft rustle of cars on the Autostrade.
A pigeon in the church tower.
If you stop and look.

Cars rushing in the busy Rome street,
Flies flying around the wonderful food that you eat.
The gentle giggle of two moms overlooking Tuscany
and an angry farmer climbing a hill.
If you stop and hear Italy.

You will see a man and woman struggling up a hill
in a three wheeled car.
The picturesque countryside, two children playing on
the steps of an Etruscan museum.
People walking arm in arm to help the elderly into a
beautiful cathedrale.
You will see thousands of years of art, history, and
pride captured at every turn.
You will see beauty.
If you stop and learn.

If you stop and taste Italy,
you will never forget the pastas, sauces, and gelato.
If you just take the time to stop.

If Only for a Moment

A first born son makes a difference in our lives
If only for a moment

You touched our hearts in many ways
I touched your heart as well

With your caring smile and warm embrace
Each moment has a story to tell

You made me realize life beyond my own
A difference only you could make

A beautiful human with a perfect soul
A snapshot of life you could take

You will never know the joy you brought
Just by being you

The many lessens you also taught
With your heart that is true

I treasured every moment
I wish I could make each one last

Your soul has a different purpose
Another meaningful task

I am thankful for the time I had
Even though it was just a moment

You'll never know the difference that moment made.

How to Make a Difference

Do you ever wonder
what a difference your life will make
Do you go over every bad thing or each tiny mistake

Without realizing the difference you make
just by being who you are
By taking in each moment and reaching for the stars

By being a person who's genuine and sincere
Taking time to appreciate and love those who are near

Doing to others as you'd wish done to you
Holding steadfast to a faith that'll always be true

Smiling at all of life's little quirks
Taking pride in your family and your wife at work

Providing inspiration with courage, comforting tears
Knowing your friends and family will always be near

By being a person who lives life as an example to lead
You and your family will always have strength
and never a need

If you ever wonder
what a difference you make in the life you have
Just know, you have made a positive impact
By being a great husband, friend, son and Dad

Faith

Why are we here, what is this life about
Why am I struggling, does no one care if I shout
Is there more meaning to my everyday
Does it really matter if I chose the right way

Yes

There is a heavenly spirit in the world above
With open arms filled with comfort and love
With an understanding of you,
yourself you do not know
With infinite opportunities to learn and grow

Listen

Faith means trusting there is more to life
There is a purpose in being good
and honoring your wife
There is someone you can talk to when no one cares
There are ways to mend a life full of tears

Hope

When you do for another, it helps your own soul
Look beyond yourself and the things you know
Fill your heart with compassion for others
Take time to listen to your father and mother

Wisdom

Look for purpose and meaning in the world around
When you focus on helping others
your own soul is found
I am here just look into the sky
There is more to your life than watching
the world pass by

Faith

For Today: September 11, 2001

In time of reflection, in time of need
One thinks of those for which she would bleed

She thinks of the strength given to her everyday
The love she shares that will never go away

She thinks of the friends who have made her smile
Of the family who've stood beside her all the while

Of the many days filled with fun and laughter
Of the days of sorrow that wasn't ever after

Of the people around her who do not give up
Of those who unselfishly help fill her cup

Of those to whom she looks forward to saying,
"Well Hello!"
Those to whom she has lost touch
and whose lives she does not know

Of all that have made her the person she has become
She is filled with love, appreciation,
and that is not done

She thanks you for each and everyday you share
She just wanted to let you know, she truly cares

Everyday

Everyday I get to know you just a little more
I am amazed
Everyday I love you even more
The road we pave

Everyday I hear your laughter
My spirits start to rise
Everyday I feel your sorrow
I love being by your side

Everyday I treasure the wonderful man
I have found
Everyday I appreciate you more
I try to not let you down

Everyday I am true
Loyal and sincere
Everyday I am thankful
You will always be here

Everyday I love you
More than words can describe
When I think of you
My heart fills with pride

Thank you for your love
The treasure of your heart
Thank you for your kindness
An honest sincere start

Happiness

What does it take to say "I am happy today!"
Is it a brand new car or traveling a world away?

Or is it something a little more
By doing for another without keeping score

Is it taking in every moment of a life that is new
Sharing in their joy and smiling at every view

Seeing the ones you love hold him near
Thinking everything is a miracle in your precious dear

Enjoying the day and all that is in it
Seeing in another their goodness a strong spirit

Taking in the moments you have
Appreciating, little time for the bad

Knowing you are good for who you are
Helping another reach their own star

A Life Worth Living

My existence may have been meager
in the minds of some
But, when it came to a fighting spirit
I definitely had one

With arthritic hands and feet, swollen and sore
I cleaned and worked, until I could work no more

I cooked meals that were beyond compare
I took pride in myself, especially in my hair

I found joy in the animals I fed
I especially liked the color of red

I cared for others, my greatest achievement of all
No one can claim that I never stood tall

Even though I loved my time here on earth
I am now in a place that truly knows my worth

I am so happy to be the person I am
And that I'll never walk in pain again

Thank you to all who shared my life
To my husband, I am thankful to be your wife

My heart goes out to all of you
Be reassured I now have a heavenly view

My Wish For You

In Life's Journey,
there are many who come in and out of your life
My wish for you is time and energy are spent on those
who add meaning, build you up, and help make the
world better

For those who have given you sorrow
My wish for you is for you to throw a stone into the
ocean for each one, watch the waves wash over them,
and let them go

For the challenges that lie ahead
My wish for you is you can face them straight on, and
come out, like you always do, victorious

For those who are caught up in materialism
My wish for you is to always
stand up for what is right, hold your head high:
people are mean when they are jealous

For those who have always loved and supported you
My wish for you is you always
keep them in your thoughts
Take time for those who love you

For the one who unconditionally loves you
My wish for you is that you hold on
and cherish every second
True love is a gift, always treat him that way

For a busy world
My wish for you is to slow down and enjoy
Life is better when you take time for you

For a beautiful woman with a tenacious spirit
My wish for you is to take the best from the past, to
stop and enjoy the present,
and to never be afraid of the future

You are admired and loved

The Value of a Dime

What is the 'Value of a Dime'?
Is it clothes, a car, or spending time?

Does it mean that you will increase your wealth,
Or that you will help others gain their health?

Take a moment to think what value means to you
Does the value of a dime help make your dreams come true?

Does the value you see come from within?
Smiling, helping others, and making that win!

Value is expressed in many different ways
Let's talk value to help brighten others days!

I Believe in You

I believe in you
I believe in your strength
It will carry you through

I believe in your attitude
Your ability to see the good

I believe in your best
Doing the things you know you should

I believe in your beauty
On the inside as well as out

I believe in your enthusiasm
To make others go and shout

I believe in your success
In whatever you set out to do

I believe in your priorities
Make life what is important to you

I believe in your uniqueness
The combination you bring is great

I believe in your heart
Make happiness your state

I believe you will make life the best it can be
You truly are remarkable
Thank you for believing in me!

How to Measure the Life of a Man

A wise woman said, to measure the life of a man
It is not by the size of his wallet or hand,
but by the size of his heart

A man's worth is not measured by his clothes, car, or
having traveled so far
But by being able to hold back
words that are tart

His happiness is not measured by his success alone,
But also by helping others build a happy home
and truly caring

By being kind to those who are dear
Giving a helping hand to those who are near
And always sharing

Worth is not measured by the size of his thoughts
By his many tumbles or size of his knots
But rather by his deeds

Worth is a measure of kind words, actions, and
conversation
Being proud to protect our nation
Helping others fulfill their needs

A man who can live his life by reaching others
Helping children, sisters and brothers
Has truly lived

Thank you for always being there
Weathering skies that were not fair
You are a special gift

Biographies

Patsy S.C. Jud

Since a young girl, Patsy has had the ability to reflect on life events through poetry. Many of the poems shared here are a result of an event in her life or the life of someone close to her. Patsy is thankful she is able to bring comfort through her words.

Patsy enjoys and is proud to present motivational talks. She delivers acclaimed talks on *The Power of a Positive Attitude* and *Pride Makes a Difference* and is able to create speeches that fit an organization's needs. She is a certified Toastmaster. Patsy S.C. Jud, MBA, BS, is the daughter of William Von and Alice Chamberlain of Wyoming. Patsy currently lives in Michigan with her husband, Brad, and their two sons.

Kenneth F. Hilliard

Ken developed his interest in the photographic arts while attending the University of Florida. In addition to his studies in Chemistry, Ken took courses in art and discovered an aptitude for constructing works in different media. Receiving blue ribbons for his early photographs of nature, he was motivated to develop an evolving understanding of how light affects the dynamics of a photograph. Ken has also expanded his work in the visual arts through the medium of stained glass, which he has enjoyed as a hobby for several years. He was born and raised in West Palm Beach, Florida, currently lives near Atlanta with his wife of 33 years and has a son who lives in Michigan.

If you have a poetry request
or would like Patsy to talk to your organization on *The Power of a Positive Attitude*,
please contact Ms. Jud at: patsyjud@yahoo.com

Please visit our web site at
http://InspirationWhenYouNeedIt.com
to order additional copies of this book or to contact the authors.